STEEL THUNDER
ON THE EASTERN FRONT

STEEL THUNDER
ON THE EASTERN FRONT
German and Russian Artillery in WWII

STACKPOLE BOOKS
TEXT BY MICHAEL OLIVE

STACKPOLE
BOOKS

Copyright © 2014 by Stackpole Books

Published in 2014 by
STACKPOLE BOOKS
5067 Ritter Road
Mechanicsburg, PA 17055
www.stackpolebooks.com

Cover design by Caroline M. Stover
Photos from a private collection

Printed in the United States of America

10 9 8 7 6 5 4 3 2 I

Library of Congress Cataloging-in-Publication Data

Olive, Michael.
  Steel thunder on the Eastern Front : German and Russian artillery in World War II / Stackpole Books ; text by Michael Olive.
    pages cm. — (Stackpole military photo series)
  Includes bibliographical references.
  ISBN 978-0-8117-1209-5
  1. World War, 1939–1945—Artillery operations, German. 2. World War, 1939–1945—Artillery operations, Soviet. 3. World War, 1939–1945—Campaigns—Eastern Front—Pictorial works. I. Stackpole Books (Firm) II. Title.
  D757.5.O45 2014
  940.54'130947—dc23
                              2014031599

CONTENTS

INTRODUCTION

Artillery: the king of battle, the most lethal killing instrument on the battlefield. Artillery fire is estimated to be responsible for 70 percent of the infantry casualties in World War II. By contrast, small-arms fire caused only about 1 percent of total casualties.

Both the fragmentation and blast effect of high-explosive shells are lethal to unprotected infantry. Even deep entrenchments and reinforced bunkers are vulnerable to the variety of specialized shells employed.

The science of artillery—both the weapons themselves and the way they were employed—improved markedly during World War I, due to the massive artillery duels taking place primarily on the Western Front. The caliber of the weapons increased and artillery tactics became far more sophisticated.

Initially, barrages before offensives were massive, with hundreds of thousands of rounds fired over several days. Later in the war, artillery became less of a blunt instrument and was used with more precision and finesse. Creeping barrages protected advancing infantry and counter-battery artillery duels were common, with ranging and identification of enemy batteries becoming increasingly effective.

The end of the war saw both Germany and Russia economically ruined and in a state of political upheaval. The Treaty of Versailles imposed severe restrictions on the size of the German Army, both in terms of numbers of troops and in the type, number, and size of weapons allowed.

The armaments industry was also thrown into disarray with the two principal manufacturers of artillery, Krupp and Rheinmetall, limited in the types of guns they could produce. Krupp was restricted to weapons above 17cm caliber and Rheinmetall to weapons below 17cm. In addition, only a small number of guns of the permitted calibers were allowed to be produced.

These restrictions were avoided when Krupp came to an arrangement with Bofors of Sweden, and Rheinmetall set up a company in Switzerland called Waffenfabrik Solothurn AG. Bofors acquired all of the foreign rights to Krupp-designed guns and Krupp sent a number of its designers to work in the Bofors factory. Rheinmetall designs originating in the design office based in Germany were manufactured in Sweden and marketed as Solothurn weapons.

When the National Socialist Party came to power in Germany in 1933, this pretense was immediately dropped. Soon the great factories in the Ruhr were churning out masses of weapons once more.

In the interwar years, all nations were looking for basically the same thing when it came to artillery: effective, robust, and standardized weapons. In the case of the *Wehrmacht* at the beginning of the war, artillery equipment was standardized on a few calibers, and the guns were well designed and reliable, having been tested extensively. The standard army field artillery were in 10.5cm, 15cm, and 21cm calibers. In order to simplify production, maintenance, and supply, a gun of a particular caliber and a howitzer (designed with a higher elevation) of the next higher caliber had interchangeable gun carriages. Antiaircraft defense relied on the 2cm and 3.7cm light guns, the 8.8cm medium gun, and the 10.5cm heavy gun. The standard antitank gun was the 3.7cm and the 7.92mm antitank rifle was provided for infantry use.

However, the experience of combat soon disrupted this tidy arrangement. Initially, the campaigns in Poland, France, and Greece did nothing to challenge the German belief that their artillery was the best in the world, although the effectiveness of the 3.7cm *PaK 36* against heavy French and British tanks was soon called into question. With the invasion of the Soviet Union on 22 June 1941, this illusion was shattered.

The Soviet Army Command decided on 76mm as the caliber of the light divisional gun, 122mm for the heavy divisional gun, and 152mm for the heavy howitzer (primarily a corps or army asset). Antiaircraft guns were of 76mm and 85mm calibers. The antitank guns were of 45mm and 57mm calibers. All of these guns were well designed, robust, and offered a good ballistic performance.

To their consternation, the Germans soon came to realize that Red Army artillery weapons were not only in no way inferior to their German counterparts but also in most cases more lightweight with longer ranges. Although the standard Soviet divisional guns fired a lighter round than their German equivalents, this was not as disadvantageous as some might assume.

Fortunately for the Germans, huge numbers of Soviet artillery pieces were captured in the first six months of the war and eagerly accepted into the German inventory. Soon entire *Wehrmacht* artillery regiments were equipped with captured weapons. There was usually enough captured ammunition to meet requirements, but in the case of the excellent 122mm M-1938 gun, the Germans produced over 1 million shells.

In response to perceived shortcomings, the German High Command demanded new guns with increased range and reduced weight. However, in assuming the war would be of short duration many promising artillery designs were abandoned, as they could not be brought into service within a year. This was a serious error as it required substantial resources and effort to try to make up for the time lost.

A good case in point was the shock caused by the appearance of the T-34 and KV-1 tanks. The standard German 3.7mm *PaK 36* antitank gun was completely useless against these vehicles. The 50mm *PaK 38* was just coming into service but was only capable of destroying these tanks at short ranges of 500 meters or less. Consequently, the potent 75mm *PaK 40*, in development since 1939, was ordered to be urgently brought into service and the first guns were issued in November 1941.

The Soviets did not make the same error, continuing to improve existing guns as well as designing and producing excellent new weapons. The provision of vast amounts of equipment to the Soviet Union by the Allies allowed Soviet industry to largely concentrate on weapons production.

The German Army experienced the devastating power of Soviet artillery during the murderous battle at Stalingrad and the subsequent Soviet counteroffensive. Massed Red Army artillery blunted German infantry and tank attacks, and supporting artillery on the opposite bank of the Volga could shell German positions with impunity as counter-battery fire could not reach the Soviet guns.

In July 1943 the *Wehrmacht* tried to regain the initiative on the Eastern Front by launching Operation Citadel, a massive assault on the bulge around the city of Kursk. The Germans were comprehensively outgunned by the Red Army by a factor of 2 to 1.

The *panzer* divisions faced a veritable wall of antitank and field guns and dug-in tanks deployed in depth. After ten days of battering through successive defense lines, the offensive was called off on the express order of Adolf Hitler. Although not the catastrophic defeat that the Soviets claimed, this was the first German summer offensive that was decisively stopped.

From that time on the Soviets held the initiative, with each new offensive preceded by a malestrom of artillery fire. As the German artillery became weaker, the Soviet artillery became stronger.

For Operation Berlin in April 1945 the Soviet front-line artillery strength consisted of 15,654 field guns of 76mm caliber and above, 4,520 antitank guns, 15,181 mortars, 3,255 rocket launchers, and 3,411 antiaircraft guns. Artillery density was an unprecedented 1 gun every 13 feet.

GERMAN FIELD ARTILLERY

The standard light field howitzer of the German Army was the *10.5cm leichte Feldhaubitze 18*, designed by Rheinmetall in 1929–30 and introduced into service in 1935. Reliable and sturdy, it remained in service throughout the war.

A pair of whitewashed *10.5cm le FH 16* guns. Though relics of World War I, their performance was adequate and, more to the point, necessary to equip units lacking artillery.

The *le FH 18* fired a standard high-explosive shell weighing 14.8 kilograms (32.7 pounds) to a maximum range, with charge number 6, of 10,675 meters (11,675 yards). The ammunition is in two pieces: the shell itself and the cased charge. It was common for artillery batteries to set up near buildings for both cover and shelter, especially during the brutal winter months.

A hastily constructed field position for the *le FH 18*, with the full gun crew and what is most likely the battery commander. The ready supply of ammunition is in the wooden boxes in the foreground.

A 10.5cm gun hidden under the guise of a peasant hut. Although not so necessary in the early years of the campaign, after 1943 the resurgent Red Air Force, operating mainly in a ground support role, made life very difficult for concentrations of German artillery.

An early model of the 10.5cm howitzer *le FH 16*, a World War I design. It was the standard field howitzer of the new *Wehrmacht* artillery regiments until 1939.

The *10.5cm le FH 18* fired a high-explosive shell and an antitank round *10cm Pzgr rot* capable of penetrating 62mm of armor at 1,000 meters. The antitank round was fired with charge 5. Also used was a hollow charge round *10.5cm Gr 39 rot Hl/A* capable of penetrating 100mm of 90-degree armor, fired with charge 5 or 6.

An *le FH 18* at the moment of firing. It came as somewhat of a shock to the German High Command that as good as the *le FH 18* was, it was significantly outranged by the Soviet 76mm field gun and the British 25-pounder at 13,580 meters (14,850 yards) and 12,250 meters (13,400 yards), respectively.

Setting up a firing position with some rudimentary camouflage. It took about forty minutes to prepare the *le FH 18* for firing.

In order to provide some protection from air attack, guns and vehicles were often situated next to trees, buildings, and, in this instance, a haystack. This *le FH 18* has the cast steel wheels associated with horse-drawn guns.

Three guns of a *10.5cm le FH 18* undergoing routine maintenance. The artillery regiment fielded three light units, each comprising a staff battery and three batteries of four guns for a total of thirty-six *le FH 18s*.

A light howitzer battery in action. Note the wide spacing between each gun to minimize the effect of counter-battery fire. The gunners are wearing their camouflaged shelter quarters. The *le FH 18* fired four to six rounds per minute.

Aiming an *le FH 18* with the sliding breech block evident. The officer on the left is carrying a leather map case and the soldier on the right has a packet for a gas cape next to his gas mask canister, an item soon discarded as the threat of gas attack diminished. In the extreme case of operating in an antitank role, the gun would be sighted by looking through the barrel itself.

Loading an *le FH 18*. The relatively light weight of the projectile and the cased charge is evident. The rammer ensures that the shell is properly seated.

The gravesite of a 10.5cm gun grew. The bodies of German soldiers killed in action were not sent home, but instead buried in cemeteries near where they fell. The use of birch to mark their graves was a common German practice, as was the placing of the helmet on the marker or the grave itself.

An *le FH 18* photographed with its barrel at full recoil. The recoil system of the *le FH 18* consisted of a buffer contained in the cradle and the hydropneumatic recuperator placed above the barrel. A hydropneumatic balancing press was placed below the cradle as a counterbalance for the muzzle's heaviness, thereby making the gun layers' task easier.

In contrast to the gunners in the previous photograph, this gun crew is well equipped for winter with specialized padded clothing, placing this scene in the winter of 1942–43.

A good view of a dug-in 150mm gun position with ready-use ammunition close by. The aiming stakes in the right background are used for calibrating the sights.

An *le FH 18* partially dug in for use in the defensive direct-fire role. The soldier in the foreground is wearing the coveted sheepskin coat, usually issued for guard duties in extreme cold. During the almost disastrous winter of 1941–42, divisional artillery was tightly integrated with German defensive positions.

Preparing for indirect fire on enemy positions. In an effort to increase the range of the *le FH 18*, later models were fitted with a muzzle brake and modified recoil system. Firing a special long-range shell with a special charge increased maximum range to 12,230 meters (13,479 yards). The improved howitzer was designated *10.5cm le FH 18M.*

Troops unload shells and charges for a 10.5cm gun. The shells are in the wood frames while the gunpowder charges are in the wicker cases.

A thoroughly burnt 10.5cm gun. Although it appears relatively intact, the metal would have undergone significant stresses and is now only suitable for scrap.

During the retreats of the winter of 1941–42, many *le FH 18* had to be abandoned because of a lack of towing vehicles to move them. The horse-drawn limbers were unable to extricate them from deep snow. The *Wehrmacht* then began a massive redesign program to simplify and lighten its artillery while also developing prime movers like the *Maultier* (mule) half-track seen here that were better suited to snow and mud conditions.

A nice view of an *le FH 18* being readied for firing. The protective muzzle cap is clearly visible. The maximum elevation was 40 degrees.

An army on the move is a difficult thing to supply, especially in Russia as the weather turned. Troops were not above looting in order to survive.

A well dug-in and camouflaged *le FH 18* with slit trenches for protection of the crew. Russian counter-battery fire was usually very accurate and heavy.

Roughly translated as "Keep dust down, enemy has this area under watch," this sign is an important reminder that Russian artillery was only an errant dust cloud away.

A very exposed *le FH 18* battery in open country. The ready supply of ammunition is evident.

It took a team of six horses and two drivers to tow the *10.5cm le FH 18*. In many instances, particularly during the spring thaw, horses were better able to move equipment and supplies than motor vehicles.

A proud and skilled artillerist (as denoted by the Gunner's Proficiency badge on his left sleeve) poses against his 10.5cm gun.

Trucks were not intended to tow artillery, but this sometimes occurred in the case of lighter guns such as 5cm antitank guns and the *le FH 18*.

A horse-drawn *le FH 18* and its limber. As the 10.5cm howitzer was relatively easy to aim, it was often used as an antitank gun when Soviet tank units broke through German lines. An antitank round was provided for the *10cm Pzgr rot* that could penetrate 56mm of armor at 30 degrees from vertical at 500 meters.

A *10cm schwere Kanone 18* with solid aluminum wheels for horse-drawn transport in two loads. The 10cm gun was judged to have too little performance for its size and production was terminated in 1943.

A *10cm sK 18* gun and limber, whitewashed to match the winter conditions of 1944, in the open.

The impressive sight of a *15cm schwere Feldhaubitze 18* battery in action. It has been positioned in a depression that prevents Russian spotters from observing it. Nonetheless, the likelihood of Russian counter-battery fire meant the German battery would eventually change positions.

A *15cm s FH 18* being towed by the *Sd.Kfz. 7*, the standard tow vehicle for this howitzer. The towing capacity of this vehicle was eight tons. Although the German half-tracks were fairly complex vehicles, they had outstanding cross-country performance.

Another view of at least two s FH 18 batteries ready for action.

The standard heavy howitzer of divisional artillery for the German Army in World War II, the *15cm schwere Feldhaubitze 18*. The *s FH 18* had a maximum range of 13,250 meters (14,490 yards) and a sustained rate of fire of up to four rounds a minute. Its separately cased shells weighed 43.5 kilograms (96 pounds), and the artillery piece required a crew of twelve. Although outclassed in terms of range by some Allied heavy artillery, the reliable and effective *s FH 18* was produced throughout the war, although demand always exceeded supply.

Catastrophic failure of the barrel section closest to the breech. Luckily the shell did not explode, or there would have been little left of the gun.

Often difficult to distinguish, a 10cm gun reveals its longer and more slender barrel compared to the shorter and beefier barrel of the 15cm.

This howitzer is positioned for either direct fire on identified enemy positions or for use in the antitank role.

Fusing shells. Wearing very casual clothing usually indicates a front-line position where uniform regulations were far more relaxed.

A dramatic shot of the business end of a heavy howitzer.

Chains have been fitted to the wheels to improve traction in the snow. The *s FH 18* had a long barrel for a howitzer.

Although German artillery used smokeless powder, as did Soviet artillery, the dust stirred up by firing betrayed the position of the battery. It was important for troops to prepare cover, no matter how crude, in case of counter-battery fire.

An *s FH 18* being transported by rail. Given the sorry state of roads in the Soviet Union, rail transport was faster and more efficient. The crews traveled with the guns and assisted in the loading, securing, and unloading.

Note that care has been taken to cover the breeches and sensitive optical sights.

"Soup's on!" The all-important meal break, taken whenever and whenever possible.

The *s FH 18* had eight different charges of increasing power, although the firing of charges 7 and 8 required special permission to use them because of the resulting damage to the breech.

A truck of the three-ton class such as the Opel "Blitz" could tow the *s FH 18* on good roads like the one depicted here. Such paved roads were exceedingly rare in the Soviet Union.

Manhandling the *s FH 18* across a narrow bridge. The gun was quite heavy at 5.43 tons and considerable efforts were made to produce a lighter variant. The resulting *s FH 36* weighed 3.23 tons, as it had a shorter barrel and a carriage largely made of alloy. Production ceased in 1942 because of a shortage of light alloys.

An *s FH 18* and its *Sd.Kfz. 7* tow vehicle about to cross a pontoon bridge of twenty-ton capacity. The numerous waterways of the Soviet Union required engineers to construct bridges of various weight capacities.

The striped pole to the right is an aiming stake used to calibrate the on-carriage sight. The stake was placed 100 meters from the gun and the aimer zeroed the optical sight on the stake, which became the baseline for any directional changes.

The heavy battalion of the artillery regiment of an infantry division had an establishment of a staff section and three batteries, each with four *s FH 18* for a total of twelve of the heavy howitzers.

A horse-drawn team takes a break, while in the background the barrel of an *s FH 18* is transported to the front. The gun's carriage was carried as a separate load.

The long barrel of the *s FH 18* is quite evident in this photograph. The total length of the gun was 4.5 meters (14.75 feet).

In the *panzer* divisions the *s FH 18* was towed by a half-track in order to keep up with the tanks. The heavy artillery battalion of a *panzer* division in June 1941 usually consisted of three batteries of *s FH 18s*, each battery consisting of two gun sections with two half-tracks and two *s FH 18s* for a total of twelve guns.

The battery would soon use up its immediate supply of ammunition and the supply trucks would immediately return to the main ammunition supply point, usually located 3 kilometers behind the gun positions.

The first winter in Russia highlighted problems with German lubricants not being suitable for the conditions. In the case of artillery pieces, the major problem was the hydraulic fluid in the recoil buffers freezing. This was rectified in the winter of 1942–43.

A good example of the firing position of an *s FH 18*. In the foreground are an empty cartridge case and a container for the propellant charge. The mats under the wheels are clearly visible.

An *s FH 18* battery, with only one *Sd.Kfz. 7* tow vehicle visible, awaits transport to new positions.

The *s FH 18* on the move. The tall and dense Russian forests posed some problems for the *s FH 18*, as firing from them required the ability to do so at high elevations. The maximum elevation of Soviet heavy artillery was 63 degrees, and the *s FH 18* only 45 degrees.

Setting up the *s FH 18* for firing. The crew detaches the heavy trails from the trailer support wheels prior to spreading them into the firing position.

Above and below: The gun is in its firing position. In the photograph above, the mats under the wheels are to prevent slippage. The first shot is used to approximate range and drive the trails into the ground for added stability. After that first shot, the aimer then recalibrates the optics for accurate shooting.

Some attempt has been made to camouflage the gun by placing it next to some small trees.

The gun aimer checks his *M32/M32K* panoramic sight.

Two *s FH 18*s just after firing with the barrel at full recoil. Note there is very little smoke visible.

Left and above: An interesting series of photographs depicting an overturned *s FH 18*. It appears that the *Sd.Kfz. 7* tow vehicle tried to take the corner too sharply or at too high a speed. As usual, the incident draws a large crowd of curious spectators.

Manhandling the *s FH 18* into firing position. The pristine uniforms and relaxed attitudes indicate a training exercise.

The solid rubber tires were used for motorized transport versions. The *s FH 18* was towed in one load in this instance, enabling it to be set up for firing much faster.

Another view of the trails being lifted from the wheeled limber. When the gun was carried in two loads for horse-drawn transport, mating the barrel to the carriage was back-breaking and time-consuming work.

The gun of a mechanized/armored unit crosses one of the interminable waterways of the Soviet Union. Note the muzzle cap to protect the rifling of the barrel.

The German artillery was often hampered by a lack of ammunition because of the difficulties in bringing supplies forward and the limited industrial capacity. After 1943, Allied bombing added to the shortages of materiel.

The most commonly used shell was the high-explosive *15cm Gr 19* fused for percussion (*AZ 23v*) or time (*Dopp Z S/60*). The time delay–fused shell was fired in a flat trajectory. As it hit the ground and bounced into the air, the mechanical time fuse was activated, detonating the shell when it was about 10 meters in the air. The effect on massed infantry was devastating.

A very clear photograph of the horizontal sliding block breech mechanism, sight, and elevating/traversing mechanism of an *s FH 18*. The howitzer is at close to its maximum elevation of 45 degrees and could traverse 64 degrees left and right.

Camouflage was of paramount importance to avoid detection and subsequent Soviet counter-battery fire. Camouflage netting was used where available, and also local foliage as in the photograph above. However, as illustrated below, the Russian steppe was often devoid of cover.

An impressive array of *s FH 18s* of an armored/mechanized unit being transported by rail to the front.

A happy gun crew. The *s FH 18* required a crew of twelve and one gun commander. As there are sixteen soldiers in the photograph, it is likely that the battery commander and some support staff have joined in.

The *s FH 18* was certainly impressive to look at but not a particularly outstanding weapon. It was of entirely conventional design, overbuilt for its role, and outranged by most Soviet and Allied artillery. However, for the German Army the major problem of the *s FH 18* was that there were never enough of them available.

The *s FH 18* at full recoil. The concussion and noise from firing was considerable for all heavy artillery pieces and most gunners suffered some form of hearing loss.

Part of an *s FH 18* battery hastily deployed on a road.

Water-soluble whitewash was used to camouflage artillery in winter. It was washed off in the spring.

Using snow and ice to provide some protection for the guns. Digging into the frozen ground was not possible by hand; crews had to use mechanical means or explosives. In the left of photograph above, a bunker has been constructed from snow.

This page and the next: Spectacular shots of an *s FH 18* being fired at night. The huge muzzle flash from the escaping propellant made it very easy for Soviet flash-ranging equipment to detect the gun positions.

The low elevation indicates direct fire on relatively close targets. Obviously something substantial has been hit.

Caught just at the moment of firing, the exertion on the gunner's face is very apparent.

A well-situated *s FH 18* in the midst of trees and shielded behind buildings. In this position the gun could only be used for indirect-fire missions.

The shell is loaded and the gun aimer checks his *M32* sight, designed for laying in both direct and indirect fire. The *M32* was a 4x power unit with a 10-degree field of view.

The *s FH 18* in its single-load towing configuration.

Two good examples of the *s FH 18* and its *Sd.Kfz. 7* tow vehicle. The maximum road speed of the *Sd.Kfz. 7* was 50 kilometers per hour (31 miles per hour). The bridge looks barely capable of handling the weight.

The attempt at camouflage is of dubious utility in the barren landscape.

Members of an *s FH 18* gun crew somewhat self-consciously pose for a photograph. The condition of their uniforms and the pristine look of the gun suggest a recent posting to the front.

Another view of the *M32/M32K* panoramic sight. Gun laying was quite a complex and technical process.

The maximum range of the "88" in the ground role was 14,815 meters (16,202 yards). German light and medium *Flak* guns were often tightly integrated into defensive positions. The standard *8.8cm Spgr Patr L/4.5* high-explosive round was used in the ground role, but percussion rather than time fused.

The importance of radio communication between artillery observers and the artillery positions farther back was paramount in supplying the front-line infantry with timely and accurate artillery support.

An 8.8cm *Flak* on over-watch duty, capable of dealing with the majority of Allied tanks at long range throughout the war.

The immensely powerful 8.8cm *PaK 43/41* antitank gun, an adaptation of the superb *PaK 43*. As the barrels of the *PaK 43* were easier to make than the gun carriage, these extra barrels were fitted to a carriage consisting of the trail legs of the *10.5cm le FH 18* and the wheels from the *15cm s FH 18*. Although the resulting gun was a highly effective tank killer that could penetrate 139mm of 30-degree slope armor at 2,000 meters, it was heavy and difficult to move and position. This led to the nickname of *Scheuntor* (barn door), given by the troops that used it in action.

GERMAN SELF-PROPELLED ARTILLERY

Panzergrenadiers hitch a ride aboard an early variant of the *Sturmgeschütz III* of *Abteilung* 197. The *Sturmgeschütz*, or *Stug*, was built on the chassis of the *Panzer III* with the intent of providing the infantry with mobile assault artillery well protected from small-arms fire as well as from some artillery and antitank weapons. Armed with a 7.5cm main gun capable of firing high-explosive and armor-piercing shells, the *Stug* would prove to be an indispensible weapon in the *Wehrmacht* throughout the war.

A side view of a *Stug III* shows its low silhouette and lack of a revolving turret. This made it harder to spot and to hit but limited the ability to engage targets to either side without turning the entire vehicle. Arguments arose within the *Wehrmacht* over whether it was better to build more *Stugs* or tanks, but as the war progressed *Stug* production increased, since they were quicker and cheaper to manufacture.

Combining the modified *Panzer II* chassis with the standard 10.5cm artillery gun created a highly mobile artillery piece that could keep pace with advancing armor. Unlike the *Stug*, however, the *Wespe* was not assault artillery and had only thin frontal armor and an open crew compartment. It was as vulnerable as regular artillery to counter-battery fire, but its ability to quickly change positions did give it an advantage.

A crewman loads the four thousandth shell into the breach of a *Wespe's* 1.5cm gun. The *Wespe* first went into combat in the spring of 1943, with over six hundred manufactured before the factory constructing them in Warsaw, Poland, was in danger of being overrun by Russian forces in the summer of 1944.

The *Grille Ausf. H* was the marriage of the Czech *LT vz. 38* chassis and the German 15cm heavy infantry gun. The *Grille* ("cricket") was yet one more expedient construction to provide German panzergrenadier units with mobile artillery. Approximately five hundred were built (*Ausf. H* and the later *Ausf. M* variant along with dedicated munitions carriers).

A *Grille* is loaded with a *Stielgranate 42*, a bunker-buster shell weighing 200 pounds. Unlike regular shells, the 42 was loaded outside the vehicle, and thus required the crew to be out of sight of enemy forces at the time.

The *Hummel* (Bumblebee) was a self-propelled 15cm howitzer mounted on the *Panzer IV* chassis. As with other self-propelled guns, it featured thin frontal armor and an open crew compartment and was allotted to *Panzer* divisions to match the speed of German armor. This particular vehicle belongs to a *Waffen SS* unit at the Battle of Kursk in July 1943.

A view of the open crew compartment. While a tarp could be rigged to protect the crew from the elements, there was no protection from shrapnel and small arms, making the *Hummel* as vulnerable as any other artillery piece.

A train load of *Sturmgeschütz* and *Sturmhaubitze*. As the war progressed and Russian armor increased in number and lethality, the German response was to up-arm the venerable *Stug* with a much longer barreled 7.5cm gun better suited to antitank duty. In addition, a 10.5cm gun was fitted to some *Stugs*, with those vehicles continuing to serve in the assault artillery role in support of the infantry.

The crew of a *Sturmhaubitze* 10.5cm assault gun celebrate the firing of their thousandth shell in combat. It is worth noting that the typical life span of a combat armored vehicle in the Second World War was most often measured in months or weeks.

A column of *Sturmhaubitze* on the Finnish Front in 1944. These particular vehicles feature the *saukopf* (pig's head) gun mantlet and the waffle-pattern *Zimmerit* antimagnetic coating, used to prevent magnetic mines from being stuck to the hull by Russian infantry.

Another view of a *Hummel*, this time behind the lines in what appears to be a training depot.

Using a mix of captured Polish and Russian armored train stock in addition to building their own, the Germans operated armored trains on the Eastern Front.

A *21cm langer Mörser* heavy howitzer, initially introduced in 1916 and modernized in the 1930s for single-load transport. Fired a 113-kilogram (249-pound) shell 11,000 meters (12,030 yards). Largely replaced in 1942 by the *21cm Mörser 18*.

A 24cm K3 heavy siege gun in position during Operation Barbarossa. Very few of these massive guns were manufactured, perhaps only fourteen in total. Their 334-pound shells were capable of hitting out to 23 miles.

The *21cm Mörser 18 Brümmbar* (Grizzly Bear), along with the *17cm K18 Matterhorn*, was the standard heavy artillery piece of the German Army in World War II. It had a maximum range of 16,700 meters (18,263 yards) and a sustained rate of fire of one round per minute. Its separately cased shells weighed 113 kilograms (249 pounds). It was designed with an ingenious dual-recoil system in which both the barrel and top carriage recoiled on firing, considerably dampening recoil stresses and thereby making the gun platform very steady. Production of the *21cm Mrs 18* ceased in 1942 with some seven hundred produced in order to concentrate on the *17cm K18*.

Some attempt has been made to camouflage these *21cm Mrs 18s*. These guns look as though they were abandoned and the barrels are in the recoil position. Perhaps their crews tried to disable them.

The impressive size of the projectile is evident. There were six increasingly powerful charges for the high-explosive shell and also six for the anticoncrete shell.

Cleaning the barrel of this massive gun was an arduous task. The *Mrs 18* weighed a hefty 16.44 tons in action.

As an army corps weapon rather than a divisional gun, it is unlikely that the *Mrs 18* was often used in the direct-fire role, as indicated by the low elevation of the barrel.

The gun crew of a *21cm Mörser 18* in a playful mood

Artillery
Proficiency Badge

Artillery
Epaulettes

Artillery Obergefreiter's
M36 Field Jacket

Artillery Officer's
Herring Bone
Twill Jacket

Artillery Officer's Field Cap

Artillery Field Cap (also called a "Crusher Cap" as the internal stiffeners have been removed)

Assault Artillery (Sturmartillerie) Field Gray Wrap Tunic

Nebelwerfer (Smoke/Rocket) Officer's Cap

Artillery Officer's M38 Overseas Cap (Feldmütze)

Smoke/Rocket Troop (Nebeltruppen) Tunic

Carl Zeiss S.F.14.Gi. H/6400
10x50 Artillery Ranging
Periscope (Scherenfernrohr)

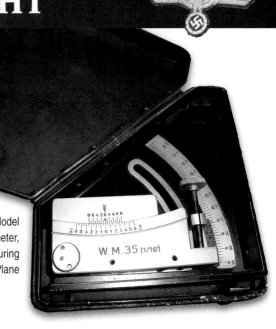

Winkelmesser Model
1935 Artillery Clinometer,
Used for Measuring
Angles in any Plane

10x80 Doppelfernrohr
(Double Telescope), Also
Known as Flak Glass (CXN
refers to Emil Busch A.G.
Rathenow Manufacturing)

Kriegsmarine
Binoculars Used for
Coastal Battery

Hensoldt Wetzlar
7X56 Binoculars
and Case

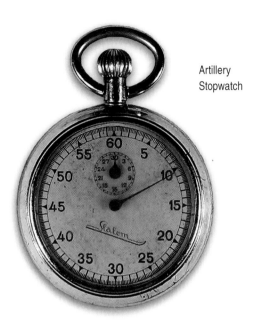

Artillery
Stopwatch

Torn.Fu. 2 Way Radio Transceiver

Artillery Theodolite For
Measuring Angles in
Both Vertical and
Horizontal Plane

Richtkreis (RKr31)-
Aiming Circle/Optical
Sighting Device for
Artillery Piece

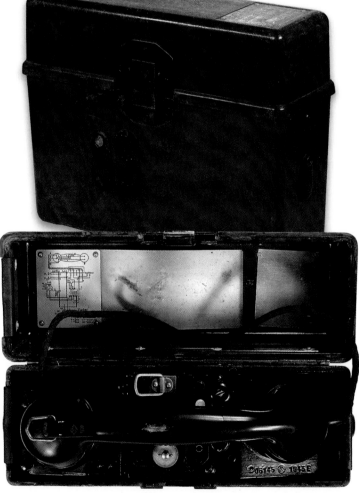

F33 1943
Field Telephone
and Bakelite Case

Wooden Case for
6 Brass 10.5cm
Brass Charges

27mm Flare
Pistol With
Colored Flares

Bakelite Artillery
Fuse Canisters

Wooden 10.5cm
Artillery Shell Cases

Tubular Steel
Artillery Shell
Canister

Explosive Charge
Cardboard Canister
for 21cm Shell

Wicker Artillery
Shell Canister

Artillery Epaulettes

Distinguished Artilleryman Badge

Lieutenant's Artillery Epaulettes (Field Uniform)

M43 Lieutenant's
Artillery
Gymnastiorka

10x45
Observation
Periscope

Artillery Mounted
Theodolite

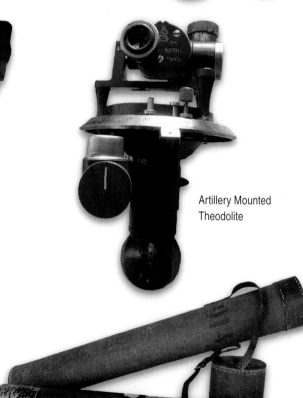

Observation
Telescope

ZOMZ (Zagorsk Optical Mechanical Plant) 6x Binoculars and Case

Artillery Fuse Container of Bakelite Material

Map Reading Compass (13x13cm Base Plate)

Field Telephone

Canvas and Leather Flare Pistol Pouch

Two Examples of Leather Exterior Map Carrying Cases

Porlammi encirclement
at Porlammi-Sommee,
5 September 1941

Finnish troops examine
captured Russian 152mm guns
in the encirclement at Porlammi,
where a large Russian force
was destroyed in the early days
of September 1941.

A German artillerist with an artistic flair
painted this rendering of his 10.5cm field
gun in the winter of 1944.

As good and effective as the *Mrs 18* was, the Army High Command decided it was not good enough to justify continued production. The *17cm K 18* fired a 62.8-kilogram (138-pound) shell a maximum distance of 29,600 meters (32,371 yards).

Limbers for the transport of the *21cm Mrs 18*.

An emplaced *21cm Mrs 18* with its aiming stakes ready for calibrating the sight.

A heavily camouflaged *Mrs 18* undergoing maintenance.

Normally the *Mrs 18* was transported in two loads: the barrel and the gun carriage. However, over short distances it could be transported in one load. The standard tow vehicle was the *Sd.Kfz 8* twelve-ton towing capacity half-track.

Numerous factors affect the trajectory of a shell: the weight of the shell, force of the charge, distance of the target, strength and direction of the wind, humidity, air temperature, and even the curvature of the earth. The gunner is consulting preprepared range tables that allow him to make the appropriate aiming corrections.

Just before firing, the gun crew prepares for the massive concussion and deafening noise by covering their ears.

The *Mrs 18* could be easily rotated through 360 degrees on its built-in turntable. Note the anchoring cables in the photograph below. This feature made it far easier to engage multiple targets.

The spectacular sight of heavy artillery firing at night. Judging by the huge flash, a powerful charge is being used. Any attempt at camouflage in this instance would be superfluous. Enemy flash-detecting equipment would be having a field day.

Two excellent views of the breech of gun "B" of a *Mrs 18* battery.

Recovering the propellant case from the breech of an *Mrs 18*. This case will be re-used with a new detonator. The gunner on the right is holding the rammer to make sure that the projectile and charge are properly seated in the breech.

The gun carriage of an *Mrs 18* ready for transport. Two *Sd.Kfz 8* half-tracks were required to move each howitzer over long distances.

A somewhat-hastily emplaced *Mrs 18* caught just at the moment of firing.

A *30.5cm Mörser (t)* and *638 (j)*, produced in 1916 and used by the Czech and Yugoslav armies in the interwar years. During the Siege of Leningrad, 1941–1944, six of these heavy mortars were used. Each shell weighed 289 kilograms (637 pounds).

The Germans used a variety of railway guns during the war, both German manufactured and captured guns—mainly French. This particular equipment is difficult to identify from this photograph but it may be a *28 cm Kanone in Eisenbahnlafette "kurz Bruno"* that fired a 240-kilogram (530-pound) shell 29,500 meters (32,260 yards).

The heavy artillery guns *17cm K18* and *21cm Mrs 18* were transported in two loads: the barrel assembly and the gun carriage. The standard towing vehicle was the *Sd.kfz 8* half-track with twelve-ton towing capacity.

GERMAN INFANTRY SUPPORT GUNS AND ROCKETS

A very interesting and unique weapon, the *7.5cm leichtes Infanteriegeschütz 18*. This was a light and handy weapon that provided the infantry regiment with a degree of organic artillery support. Each regiment was supplied with six 7.5cm light infantry guns and two 15cm infantry guns.

A battery of 7.5cm guns operated by *Waffen SS* troops in the summer of 1941 near Kokkosalmi, Kistinki, on the Finnish Front.

The unique "shotgun" breech action. The barrel was carried in a square-section casing within another casing that contained the fixed breech block and firing mechanism. Using the breech lever, the loader lifted the rear part of the barrel clear of the fixed breech block. Once it was open, the barrel was kept in place by the cartridge extractors. When the cartridge was loaded, the rim of the case forced the extractors forward, causing the barrel to release and fall forward under its own weight and thereby closing the breech.

The *7.5cm le IG 18* was easy to move, even in snow. Note the integral muzzle cap.

The *le IG 18* was so light at 405 kilograms (892 pounds) that a two-horse team could pull it, although a four-horse team was the usual configuration.

The spoke wheels indicate a horse-drawn gun. The *le IG 18* fired a 6-kilogram (13.2-pound) shell a maximum distance of 3,795 meters (4,150 yards) using charge number 5.

The crew of the *le IG 18* consisted of a gun commander, gunner, loader, and three ammunition carriers.

A good view of the simple box trail gun carriage. The somewhat-complex shield consisted of five individual parts and could be folded down.

After being superseded as an antitank gun, the *PaK 36* was sometimes used an an infantry gun, although it fired a very light shell.

Laundry day for an *le IG 18* crew. If this scene of domestic tranquility were interrupted by the enemy, the infantry gun platoon could be ready for a fire mission in approximately thirty minutes.

The heaviest weapon ever classified by any nation as an infantry gun, the *15cm schweres Infanteriegeschuutz 33*. The *s IG 33* fired a 38-kilogram (83.8-pound high-explosive shell a maximum distance of 4,700 meters (5,140 yards). It was first introduced in service in 1927, the same time as the *7.5cm le IG 18*.

Mountain troops firing a *7.5cm Gebirgsgeschütz 36*. A mountain gun introduced in 1938, it was a good design and well liked by the troops that used it. The *Geb G 36* fired a 5.75-kilogram (12.7-pound) high-explosive shell 9,150 meters (1,006 yards).

Mountain troops have fitted their *7.5cm Geb G 36* with an MG34 machine gun. The vast distances of the Russian steppes made it imperative that crews looked after their own defenses, as support was not always nearby. The addition of the MG34 would allow the crew to engage Russian infantry at close distances while saving ammunition for the main gun.

The *s IG 33* was a heavy weapon at 1.87 tons and required a six-horse team to pull it. A seven-man crew serviced the gun. The robust and reliable *s IG 33* remained in German service until 1945.

A battery of *Panzerwerfer* 42 mounting the ten-barrel 15cm *Nebelwerfer* load their tubes in preparation for a fire mission.

Rocket artillery, the distinctive smoke trails of German *Nebelwerfer* (smoke thrower) rockets. These smoke trails and the dust thrown up at launch made these weapons easily detectable and susceptible to artillery counter-battery fire, as the rockets had much shorter ranges than field artillery. Therefore, most launchers were either light and easily moved or mounted on half-track vehicles. Common German rocket calibers were 15cm, 21cm, 28cm, and 30cm.

An interesting photograph of a rocket in flight. This is either a 15cm or 21cm rocket launched from an *NbW 41* or *NbW 42* launcher barely visible at bottom left.

A *21cm Nebelwerfer 42* launcher loaded with rockets. The *NbW 42* could fire 5x 112.6-kilogram (248-pound) rockets in eight seconds and three salvos of five rockets in five minutes.

Flying artillery, a *Junkers Ju 87 Stuka* that has come to grief. Aware of their acute shortage of mobile heavy artillery, the German High Command turned to the dive bomber to provide a solution to the problem. Aircraft like the *Ju 87* were able to range far and wide over the battlefield, delivering their bombs on selected targets with a precision that the artillery could not match. In the case of the *Ju 87B* variant, up to 500 kilograms (1,100 pounds) of bombs could be carried. This scenario was all very well if almost total air supremacy was achieved. If not, the *Stuka* was slow and vulnerable to fighter attack.

The eyes of the artillery, a *Focke-Wulf Fw 189A* reconnaissance and army cooperation aircraft. This was a very successful aircraft capable of carrying out its short-range tactical reconnaissance duties efficiently. Although slow, with a top speed of only 349 kilometers per hour (217 miles per hour), the *Fw 198* was well armed with six machine guns, very agile, and able to absorb considerable punishment.

GERMAN ARTILLERYMEN

Unloading very heavy caliber shells, probably for a railway gun. It is obvious that these massive shells could not be lifted by a loader.

Preparing charges for cartridge cases, most likely for a *15cm s FH 18*. The *s FH 18* was provided with six charges of increasing power.

A captured Stalinetz S-60 artillery tractor. The Soviet artillery was well supplied with fully tracked tow vehicles.

A view of the battlefield through a gunsight. German optics were far superior to those used by the Soviets.

Catastrophic failure of what appears to be a section of barrel. Given the extreme pressures generated by firing, these sorts of failures were not uncommon, sometimes with fatal consequences for the gun crew.

Setting a nose percussion fuse.

A divisional ammunition supply dump for heavy artillery shells, a tempting target for counter-battery fire or air attack. Supply dumps were usually protected by numerous antiaircraft guns.

A *Luftwaffe* gunner sits atop his antiaircraft gun. The *grün* (green) refers to the type of hydraulic fluid used in the recuperator.

A German *Drächen* (kite) observation balloon based on the World War I design and manufactured by the Reidinger Company of Augsburg. Its normal operating height was 500 meters, providing an observation radius of 80 kilometers.

A forward observer for the artillery—an extremely hazardous task requiring technical expertise, courage, and nerves of steel.

Collecting shell casings for re-use. As with most nations, German cartridge cases were initially manufactured of solid-drawn brass. As the shortage of raw materials became more acute, various composite brass or steel cases were manufactured, and finally all-steel cases were successfully produced.

Preparing cable for a field
telephone. Orders were usually
transmitted to the artillery by
field telephone as the line was
generally secure from jamming and
interception. The serious drawback
to this system was that cables
were often cut by enemy shells,
necessitating repair under fire.

These *10.5cm le FH 18* shells make
an interesting writing desk.

Future artillery officers in training of a highly technical nature.

"Here lies the asshole of the world." Typically robust soldiers' humor, and a common sentiment among German soldiers in all areas of Russia.

A railhead supply collection point. Artillery is a prodigious user of shells, and the ready supply of light and heavy ammunition for an artillery regiment is over 6,300 shells. An ammunition supply train usually consists of thirty cars, each one loaded with fifteen tons of ammunition, generally of a specific caliber.

Removing a 15cm ammunition from its protective wicker wrapping.

A senior officer observing the battlefield with *SF 14H 6400* artillery stereo binoculars.

Luftwaffe gunners with 10x80 power *Flak* binoculars. All German optics were of exceptional quality.

Observing the battlefield in a trench that would not seem out of place in World War I. At the first sign of an enemy attack, preregistered artillery fire would be called in. German artillery was noted for its quick reaction time.

The desolate area of "no man's land." Deceptively quiet, but the enemy is always present and ready to strike. During an attack, this area becomes a deadly "kill zone" swept by artillery, machine-gun, and small-arms fire.

Engineers on both sides used captured shells as improvised mines, often wiring them in series.

Usually unexploded shells would be buried fairly deep, so this one may be a captured Soviet 122/152mm. If it were to explode, as sometimes happens unless the shell has been defused, the soldier would literally disappear.

Sighting an infantry gun with a 4x M.32 panoramic telescope. The mosquito netting was essential wear in the wet and humid Russian forests. The soldier in the background with the binoculars could be Romanian.

Observing the effect of close-range artillery fire.

An artilleryman relaxes on a horse-drawn gun limber. Five crew were carried on the limber—three at the front and two at the back. An *le FH 18* battery had a total establishment of 153 horses. Six horses were used to tow the *10.5cm le FH 18*.

A *Luftwaffe* antiaircraft gun crew operating a *Kommandohilfsgerät 35* antiaircraft director, generally used only for auxiliary purposes, with the 4-meter base range finder mounted separately. Gun data supplied by the director is normally transmitted to the guns by field telephone.

Soldiers using a theodolite, an instrument for forward observation and advanced tactical navigation, to measure angles in both the vertical and horizontal pane.

SOVIET FIELD AND HEAVY ARTILLERY

An abandoned *76.2mm Pushka obr. 1936* Soviet standard light field gun. It entered Red Army service in 1939, and was an extremely efficient field gun with excellent antitank capabilities. Its maximum range of 13,580 meters outranged the 10.5cm German standard light field gun by 3,000 meters (3,280 yards).

The long barrel indicates a high-velocity weapon, with a muzzle velocity of 706 meters per second (2,316 feet per second). The antitank capability of this gun was obvious, and the Germans converted the many captured weapons to antitank guns designated *7.62cm PaK 36(r)*. Armor penetration was 50mm at 1,000 meters. The 75mm frontal armor of a KV 1 could be penetrated at 600 meters.

The standard 1940 Rifle Division 2 artillery regiments. One was a light regiment with a battalion of 76mm guns in three batteries of four guns. Elite Guards Rifle Divisions in 1942 had three artillery battalions with two batteries of 76mm guns and one of 122mm howitzers for a total of twenty-four 76mm guns.

The standard caliber for the typical Soviet light howitzer was 76mm; for the Germans it was standardized at 10.5cm. The Soviet gun fired a lighter shell of 6.4 kilograms (14 pounds) compared to the 14.8 kilograms (32.7 pounds) of the German gun. However, it outranged the *le FH 18* by almost 3,000 meters (3,280 yards).

An improved version of the 76mm field gun the M1939 (USV), smaller, lighter, and more mobile than the 1936 model F-22. Total production was 9,812. It was superceded in 1942 by the superior 76mm ZiS-3. Captured examples were much prized by German troops; the antitank version was designated *7.62cm PaK 39(r)*. The soldier on the right carries a Soviet 7.62mm PPSh-41 machine-pistol, another Soviet weapon highly sought after by German troops.

Entire German artillery detachments were equipped with the USV, modified by the addition of a muzzle brake and designated *7.62 ck FK 297(r)*. Not only were there not enough German weapons available but also the Soviet guns were excellent weapons in their own right and lighter than their German equivalents.

A destroyed USV in position to cover a road. Of interest is that the wheels and tires were taken from the ZiS-5 truck, another example of intelligent Soviet standardization of equipment.

This appears to be an abandoned 122mm 09-30, a World War I weapon modernized in the 1930s.

A destroyed artillery position with a 152mm M1938 ML-20 and a T-26 light tank.

A captured 152mm howitzer M1938 M-10. The M-10 was designed to be the standard divisional heavy gun of the Red Army. It was introduced in 1939 but, for various reasons, production ceased in 1941. Nonetheless, the M-10 was a gun with good mobility and firepower, firing a 40-kilogram (88-pound) shell 12,400 meters (7.7 miles).

A 152mm M-10 with its STZ-3 tractor. Although production ceased in 1941, the M-10 remained in service, although in limited numbers, throughout the war.

A burned-out M-10 with its Stalinetz S-60 tow vehicle. Soviet artillery could be horse-drawn, but most were towed by tracked vehicles, placing them at a distinct advantage over their German counterparts who relied on horse-drawn guns in the line infantry divisions.

On the left is the barrel assembly of an M-20 heavy howitzer that has been broken down for transport. On the right is a 152mm 152 H 09-30, an older weapon modernized in the 1930s.

The 152mm gun-howitzer M1937 ML-20, the standard Soviet Corps/Army heavy artillery piece. This gun was an extensive upgrade to a pre-World War I Schneider design.

The ML-20 was heavier than the M-10. Until the introduction of the M1943 D-1, which combined the barrel of the M-10 and the carriage of the 122mm M-30, there were no 152mm howitzers in the division artillery assets.

More captured 152mm M-10s. Despite Soviet misgivings, the Germans considered the M-10 a highly effective weapon and impressed all serviceable guns into heavy artillery detachments.

Rather than a sliding block breech, Soviet artillery used the interrupted screw type, as it was easier to manufacture and more reliable. Seen here is the open breech of a 122mm howitzer.

The fluted muzzle brake of the ML-20 helped to divert the considerable recoil forces. The fact that the escaping gasses caused a cloud of dust at the front of the gun was a relatively minor inconvenience.

This makeshift bridge was obviously not strong enough to support the considerable weight of the ML-20, which weighed in at 7,930 kilograms (17,482 pounds) in travel configuration.

Captured ML-20s in travel configuration and trailers for the transport of heavy artillery carriages and barrels.

The ML-20 fired a 40-kilogram (88-pound) high-explosive shell a distance of 17,230 meters (18,843 yards). The German *15cm s FH 18* fired a 43-kilogram (95-pound) shell 13,325 meters (14,573 yards).

Along with the 122mm 1938 M-30, the 152mm ML-20 was captured by the hundreds as the Red Army retreated in disarray during the early months of Barbarossa. To their surprise and consternation, the Germans soon discovered that both these guns and the 76mm divisional gun were lighter and had longer ranges than their German counterparts. The short-term solution was to use as many of the Soviet guns as possible.

Despite considerable effort, the Germans never succeeded in developing a gun to match the ML-20 in terms of weight, range, and ease of production.

The main drawbacks of the ML-20 were its weight and consequent lack of mobility. From 1937 to 1945, some 6,869 guns were produced, along with 4,000 ML-20 barrels for the SU-152 and ISU-153 self-propelled guns.

An abandoned *Stalinetz* S-60 tractor and its gun, most likely a 122mm 1909/37 howitzer or a 152mm 1910/30.

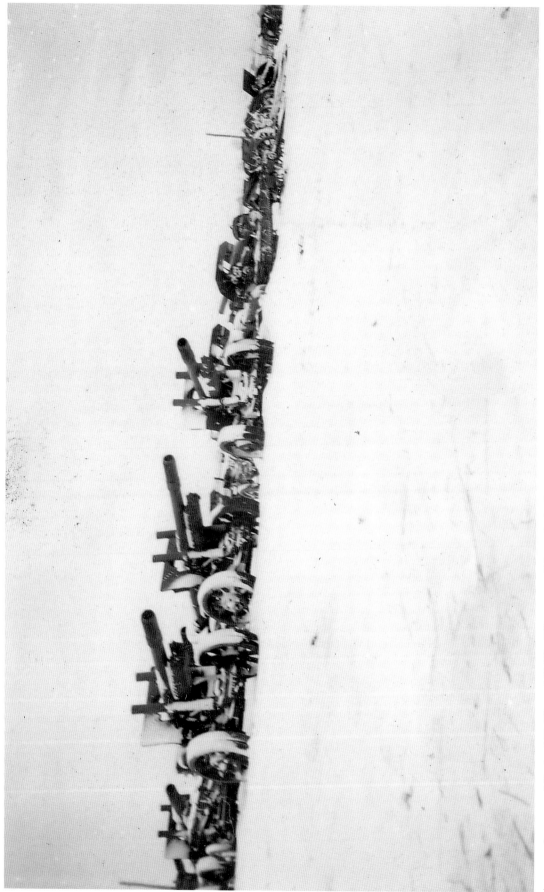

A mass of captured Soviet ML-20s and D-10s. Where possible, refurbishment would be done in the field, including the fitting of German sights in some cases.

From the start of Barbarossa to the fall of Berlin, Soviet artillery was considered particularly fearsome. The Red Army was extensively equipped with guns of all calibers and lavishly supplied with shells. In an attack, the German front-line would be deluged with artillery and mortar fire. If an attack was anticipated, the trenches closest to the enemy would be almost entirely evacuated, with the troops manning a main line of resistance farther back.

SOVIET INFANTRY GUNS, ROCKETS, AND SELF-PROPELLED GUNS

The 75mm M-31/38, the first standard Soviet heavy antiaircraft gun. The 75mm was an excellent weapon with a service ceiling of 9,300 meters (30,500 feet). In the photograph below the tow vehicle is a S-60 tractor; the antiquated German horse-drawn vehicles are in stark contrast.

Abandoned 76mm M-31s. As with many Soviet weapons, large numbers of the M-31/38 were captured in 1941 and immediately impressed into German service. These captured guns were designated *7.62 cm Flak M31(r)*.

These guns are the M-31 1931 model. Designed as a dual-purpose weapon, antitank ammunition was provided. These guns are not dug in, indicating a hasty deployment.

The 85mm M 1939 (52-K) dual-purpose gun, the Soviet equivalent of the famous German 8.8cm *Flak 18/36,* and basically a scaled-up version of the 7.62mm M-38. The vertical ceiling of this gun was 10,500 meters (34,450 feet) and the rate of fire was fifteen to twenty rounds per minute. The ceiling of the "88" was 9,900 meters (32,480 feet) and the rate of fire was fifteen rounds per minute. The barrel of the M 1939 was subsequently used in both the T-34/85 tank and the SU-100 self-propelled gun.

As with the 76mm M-31/38 the 85mm gun was eagerly taken into German service with the designation 8.5cm *Flak M 39(r).* Both the 76mm and 85mm guns were re-bored to accept 8.8cm German ammunition and issued to both home defense units and front-line forces.

This page and the next: A 76mm M 1938 battery. Heavy antiaircraft regiments consisted of sixteen guns.

Soviet antiaircraft fire was very effective, both in terms of accuracy and weight of fire.

A posed but nonetheless interesting photo of Russian infantry advancing past a ZiS 3 76.2mm gun. With simplified construction and mass production, over 100,000 were built. Capable of firing high-explosive, armor-piercing, and smoke rounds, the gun proved highly effective.

A captured 122mm howitzer with limber and STZ-3 tractor during the latter stages of Operation Barbarossa. Based on a World War I design, the 122mm was updated to include inflated rubber tires, replacing the earlier wood spokes with steel rim wheels.

A 76mm M-31 and an S-60 tractor. In December 1944 there were still 686 *7.62/8.8 Flak M31/38(r)* in German service.

The dual-purpose gun in the background appears to be a 76mm M-38, an improved version of the M-31 with a twin-axle carriage. On the right is a 152mm 1909/30 heavy howitzer.

Captured Soviet ammunition. In 1941 and 1942, vast stocks of all calibers were available, enough to meet the needs of German units using Soviet artillery for some time. In the case of many guns in widespread German service, ammunition was specifically produced in Germany or the occupied countries for these weapons. This was particularly the case for 122mm and 152mm howitzers.

The fully tracked vehicle functioning as an ammunition carrier is a STZ-3, used for towing a wide variety of guns, from antitank to heavy artillery.

Captured infantry guns and heavy artillery neatly lined up with typical German precision. The guns on the far right are 76mm 1927 model infantry guns with a useful maximum range of 8,550 meters (9,350 yards). A simple and reliable weapon, the large numbers captured were widely used by the Germans, to the extent that German sights were often fitted and special ammunition produced. The German designation was *7.62cm IKH 290(r)*.

The second most produced Soviet armored vehicle of World War II, the SU-76 combined the lengthened chassis of the T-70 light tank with the 76mm *Zis 3* gun. Serving as an infantry support vehicle, the SU-76 operated as a three-in-one weapon capable of providing indirect fire, antitank support, and serving as an assault gun.

"Captured weapon collection center. Entrance forbidden." Thousands of Soviet artillery pieces were captured in the first two years of the war. Many were scrapped, but hundreds were taken into German front-line and second-line service. Many pieces were installed on the Atlantic Wall. Some 76mm 1927 model infantry guns and older model 76mm divisional guns are apparent. In the foreground below is a 45mm PTP 1930 antitank gun, a scaled-up version of the German 3.7cm *PaK 36*.

A Soviet artillery position. Soviet troops were expert at quickly constructing elaborate fieldworks.

The superb 120mm PM-38 heavy mortar that fired a 15.6-kilogram (34.4-pound) projectile 6,050 meters (6,616 yards). The Germans were so impressed with this weapon that they produced an almost direct copy, the *12cm GrW 42*. Mortars saw widespread use on both sides.

A 203mm 1931 model B-4 heavy howitzer, an efficient heavy artillery piece produced in both wheeled and fully tracked versions. Although the gun looks self-propelled this is not the case, as it had to be towed, usually by the Voroshilovets heavy artillery tractor that used the suspension of the T-24 tank.

A panzerman of the 17th Panzer Division stands on a captured Russian 203mm howitzer in the fall of 1941. To his right is the tracked carrier for the barrel. A 152mm gun can be seen behind him.

A lineup of M-10 howitzers in the foreground; on the left are examples of the excellent 122mm M1938 (M-30) howitzer. A very successful and reliable artillery piece, it was produced in very large numbers with approximately 17,500 manufacured between 1940 and 1945. Captured weapons saw widespread German use with regular artillery detachments. The M-130 fired a 21.8-kilogram (34.4-pound) shell 12,000 meters (13,123 yards) at five to six rounds per minute.

An STZ-3 tractor with a Komsomoletz light artillery tractor in tow.

The SU-122 howitzer was a self-propelled gun that used the 122mm howitzer on the incredibly successful T-34 chassis. It first saw action in January 1943 on the Leningrad Front.

An overrun Soviet supply column. In the early days of the campaign, the swift movement of the German armored and mechanized units surprised Soviet units on a frequent basis. Even though the Red Army was far more mechanized than the *Wehrmacht*, there was still some reliance on horse-drawn transport.

A *Komsomoletz* light artillery tractor. Soviet artillery tractors were not as sophisticated as their German half-track equivalents but were more standardized and reliable.

Soviet flying artillery, the deadly *Il-2/M3 Sturmovik* heavily armored and armed with 2x23mm cannon, 2x7.62 machine-guns, and 1x12.7mm heavy machine-gun in the rear gunners position, also carried a wide variety of bombs and rockets. German soldiers nicknamed the *Il-2* "the cement truck" because it was almost impervious to small-arms fire and, more ominously, the black death. Some thirty-five thousand *Il-2s* were produced during the war.

The Russians were well versed in other mobile forms of artillery, having built armored trains during World War I. In light of the vast distances to be covered on the Eastern Front, the use of armored trains equipped with artillery proved useful on many occasions. This particular train was severely damaged and lost near Dunaburg, Latvia.

Soviet rocket projectiles. Like the Germans, the Soviets fielded a wide variety of rocket launchers and projectiles. The most common were in 82mm, 132mm, and 300mm calibers.

The 132mm M-132 rocket wighed 42 kilograms (93 pounds) with a 4.9-kilogram (11-pound) warhead. The range was 8,740 meters (9,560 yards). Usually launched from a 6x4 ZIS-6 truck, mobility was important as the launchers were easily detected and had to be moved immediately after firing to avoid counter-battery fire.

Soldiers on both sides greatly feared rocket bombardment. Rocket fire was not particularly accurate, but the saturation effect of multiple launchers was extensive and the blast effect was particularly fearsome. The Germans called the Katyusha rocket launchers "Stalin's Organ."

Self-propelled artillery, the imposing 152mm L/20 howitzer of the massive fifty-five-ton KV-2. The KV-2 was impervious to German tank and antitank gunfire. Only the 8.8cm *Flak 18/36*, heavy field guns firing over open sights, or a direct hit from a heavy bomb could destroy it.

A destroyed JSU-152 self-propelled tank destroyer. Unlike the SU-152, this version used the ML-20S gun mounted on a JS-2 chassis. It was nicknamed the *Zveroboy* ("one who fights animals") as it was capable of taking on Germany's largest tanks, including the Panther, Tiger, and King Tiger. In reality, however, its slow rate of fire and muzzle velocity meant it was not ideally suited for this task. The JSU-152 proved far more capable at serving as a bunker-buster and providing supporting fire.

The low center of gravity of the SU-152 made it far more stable than the earlier KV-2, although that came at the cost of a fixed superstructure.

The KV-2 looked more formidable than it actually was. It was excessively heavy, and coupled with a 500-horsepower diesel engine it was slow and not very maneuverable. The massive turret weighed twelve tons, rotated slowly, and would not traverse if the ground was not reasonably flat. Hull armor was very heavy for the period at 75mm for the hull and turret sides and 110mm for the turret front.

APPENDIX

Rank Comparisons

U.S. ARMY	RUSSIAN ARMY	WAFFEN-SS	GERMAN ARMY
Enlisted Men			
Private	*Krasnoarmeyets*	*SS-Schütze*	*Schütze*
Private First Class		*SS-Oberschütze*	*Oberschütze*
Corporal	*Mladshiy Serzhant*	*SS-Sturmmann*	*Gefreiter*
Senior Corporal		*SS-Rottenführer*	*Obergefreiter*
Staff Corporal		*SS-Stabsrottenführer*	*Stabsgefreiter*
Noncommissioned Officers			
Sergeant	*Serzhant*	*SS-Unterscharführer*	*Unteroffizier*
		SS-Scharführer	*Unterfeldwebel*
Staff Sergeant		*SS-Oberscharführer*	*Feldwebel*
Sergeant First Class	*Starshiy Serzhant*	*SS-Hauptcharführer*	*Oberfeldwebel*
Master Sergeant		*SS-Sturmscharführer*	*Hauptfeldwebel*
Sergeant Major	*Starshina*		*Stabsfeldwebel*
Officers			
Second Lieutenant	*Mladshiy Leytenant*	*SS-Untersturmführer*	*Leutnant*
First Lieutenant	*Leytenant*	*SS-Obersturmführer*	*Oberleutnant*
Captain	*Kapitan*	*SS-Hauptsturmführer*	*Hauptman*
Major	*Major*	*SS-Sturmbannführer*	*Major*
Lieutenant Colonel	*Podpolkovnik*	*SS-Obersturmbannführer*	*Oberstleutnant*
Colonel	*Polkovnik*	*SS-Standartenführer*	*Oberst*
Brigadier General		*SS-Brigadeführer*	*Generalmajor*
Major General	*General Major*	*SS-Gruppenführer*	*Generalleutnant*
Lieutenant General	*General Leytenant*	*SS-Obergruppenführer*	*General der Fallschirmjäger, etc.*
General	*General Armii*	*SS-Oberstgruppenführer*	*Generaloberst*
General of the Army	*Marshal Sovetskogo Souza*	*Reichsführer-SS*	*Feldmarschall*

GERMAN ARTILLERY

Type	Designation	Caliber	Weight of Shell	Rate of Fire	Armor Penetration 30 deg. from vertical	Maximum Range	Comments
Infantry Support Artillery							
7.5cm leichtes Infanteriegeschütz 18	7.5cm le IG	7.5cm/2.95in	6kg/13.23lb	8-12rpm		3,375m/3,960yd	Standard German light infantry weapon.
15cm schweres Infanteriegeschütz 33	15cm s IG 33	15cm/5.91in	38kg/83.8lb	2-3rpm		4,700m/5,140yd	Largest caliber weapon of any nation classified as an infantry gun. Overweight but very effective.
Mountain Artillery							
7.5cm Gebirgsgeschütz 36	7.5cm Geb G 36	7.5cm/2.95in	5.75kg/12.68lb	6rpm		9,150m/10,006yd	Standard light mountain gun, well liked by crews.
10.5cm Gebirgshaubitze 40	10.5cm Geb H 40	10.5cm/4.13in	14.5kg/31.97lb	4-6rpm		16,740m/18,302yd	Heaviest gun developed for mountain troops. Produced by the Austrian company Böhler. An excellent weapon.
Field Artillery							
10.5cm leichte Feldhaubitze 18	10.5cm le FH 18	10.5cm/4.13in	14.81kg/32.66lb	4-6rpm		10,675m/11,675yd	Standard light field howitzer of the German Army.
schwere 10cm Kanone 18	s 10cm K18	10.5cm/4.13in	15.14kg/33.38lb	6rpm		19,075m/20,860yd	Heavy field howitzer. Same carriage as the 15cm s FH 18.
15cm schwere Feldhaubitze 18	15cm s FH 18	15cm/5.91in	43.5kg/95.92lb	4rpm		13,250m/14,490yd	Standard heavy field howitzer of the German Army.
Heavy Artillery							
17 cm Kanone 18 in Mörserlafette (Matterhorn)		17.3cm/6.81in	62.8kg/138.47lb	1-2rpm		29,600m/32,371yd	Standard German heavy artillery piece. A Corps/Army weapon. Given a high production priority.
Lange 21cm Mörser		21.1cm/8.31in	113kg/249.2lb	1-2rpm		11,100m/12,140yd	World War I design, limited active service
21cm Mörser 18 (Brümmbar)		21.1cm/8.31in	113kg/249.2lb	1rpm		16,700m/18,263yd	Standard German heavy artillery piece. A Corps/Army weapon. Production terminated in 1942 in favor of the 17cm K18 that had almost twice the range.
Railway Artillery							
15cm Kanone in Eisenbahnlafette	15cm K (E)	14.93cm/5.88in	43kg/94.82lb	1-2 rounds every 5 min		22,500m/24,606yd	Eighteen produced to 1938. 15cm considered too small a caliber for a railway mounting.
28cm Kanone 5 in Eisenbahnlafette	28cm K 5 (E)	28.3cm/11.14in	255.5kg/563.8lb	1 round every 5 min		62,180m/68,000yd	28 produced by 1945. Standard German railway gun, one of the best to enter service.
Antiaircraft/Dual-Purpose Artillery							
2cm Flugabwehrkanone 30/38	2cm Flak 30/38	20mm/0.79in	305gm/10.67oz	120rpm practical 180-220rpm practical		Ceiling 2,000m/6,562ft Ground 1,600m/1,750yd	Standard light antiaircraft gun, also used in the ground role. Flak 38 was a modification to increase the rate of fire.
2cm Flakvierting 38	2cm Flak 38	20mm/0.79in	305gm/10.67oz	700-800 practical		Ceiling 2,000m/6,562ft Ground 1,600m/1,750yd	4-barrel version, very effective weapon. 3,851 produced.

Note: Armor penetration figures are for standard armor-piercing, high-explosive shells (APHE), not tungsten core, discarding sabot ammunition.

GERMAN ARTILLERY *continued*

Type	Designation	Caliber	Weight of Shell	Rate of Fire	Armor Penetration 30 deg. from vertical	Maximum Range	Comments
Antiaircraft/Dual-Purpose Artillery continued							
3.7cm Flugabwehrkanone 36/37	3cm Flak 36/37	37mm/1.46in	635gm/22.39oz	80rpm practical		Ceiling 4,800m/15,749ft Ground 6,685m/7,201yd	Standard light antiaircraft gun, also produced in a twin-gun mounting.
8.8cm Flugabwehrkanone 18/36/37	8.8cm Flak 18/36/37	88mm/3.36in	9.4kg/20.73lb	15rpm	1,000m–105mm	Ceiling 9,900m/32,482ft Ground 14,815m/16,202yd	Standard heavy antiaircraft gun, the feared "88." Also very effective in the antitank role.
8.8cm Flugabwehrkanone 41	8.8cm Flak 41	88mm/3.36in		20rpm	1,000m–202 mm	Ceiling 15,000m/49,215ft Ground 19,735m/21,582yd	Rheinmetall-Borsig design of an improved 8.8cm gun. Problems with cartridge extraction, but a highly effective weapon.
Antitank Artillery							
2.8cm schwere Panzerbüchse 41	2.8cm PzB 41	28mm/1.1in tapering to 20mm/0.79in	131gm/4.62oz	N/A	100m–69mm 500m–52mm	500m/547yd	Revolutionary taper bore gun, squeezing projectile to a smaller caliber for increased muzzle velocity.
3.7cm Panzerabwehrkanone 36	3.7cm PaK 36	3.7cm/1.46in	0.68kg/1.5lb	N/A	100m–68mm 500m–40mm	500m/547yd	Standard German antitank gun at the start of the war, highly mobile. Design copied by many nations.
4.2cm Panzerjägerkanone 41	4.2cm PJK 41	4.2cm/1.6in tapering to 29.4mm/1.16in	336gm/11.85oz	N/A	100m–90mm 500m–72mm	1,000m/1,094yd	Second taper bore weapon in service. Used the carriage of the PaK 36. Production terminated in 1942.
5cm Panzerabwehrkanone 38	5cm PaK 38	5cm/1.97in	2.25kg/4.96lb	N/A	500m–61mm 1,000m–50mm	1,500m/1,640yd	Replacement for PaK 36. Could only deal with T-34 and KV-1 at short ranges. In service throughout the war.
7.5cm Panzerabwehrkanone 40	7.5cm PaK 40	7.5cm/2.95in	6.8kg/14.99lb	N/A	500m–104mm 1,000m–89mm	1,800m/1,968yd	Standard antitank gun from November 1942. A powerful if somewhat heavy gun. Capable of dealing with all Allied tanks.
7.5cm Panzerabwehrkanone 41	7.5cm PaK 41	7.5cm/2.95in tapering to 5.5cm/2.17in	2.95kg/5.71lb	N/A	500m–171mm 1,000m–145mm	2000m/2,187yd	Production ceased after 150 guns produced due to a shortage of tungsten for the ammunition. Very powerful and light weapon.
7.5cm Panzerabwehrkanone 97/38	7.5cm PaK 97/38	7.5cm/2.95in	6.8kg/14.99lb	N/A	500m–55mm 1,000m–40mm	1,500m/1,422yd	French 75mm 1987 model barrels fitted to PaK 38 carriage as an expedient weapon. Low muzzle velocity and unstable when fired.
7.62cm Panzerabwehrkanone 36(r)	7.62cm PaK 36(r)	7.62cm/3.00in	7.54kg/16.63lb	N/A	500m–120mm 1,000m–108mm	1,800m/1,968yd	A modification of the Soviet 1936 model field gun. Chamber rearmed to fit a standard PaK 40 cartridge case and a muzzle break added. Used on all fronts, a very effective and efficient gun.
8.8cm Panzerabwehrkanone 43	8.8cm PaK 43	8.8cm/3.46in	10.4kg/22.93lb	N/A	500m–207mm 1,000m–190mm 2,000m–159mm	3,500m/3,828yd	An exceptional antitank gun based on the Flak 41, entered service in 1943. The cruciform mount allowed a low profile of less than 6 feet from top of shield to ground. Best antitank gun of the war.
8.8cm Panzerabwehrkanone 43	8.8cm PaK 43	8.8cm/3.46in	10.4kg/22.93lb	N/A	500m–207mm 1,000m–190mm 2,000m–159mm	3,500m/3,828yd	Expedient solution when barrel production exceeded that of the carriage. Wheels from the 15cm s FH 18 and trail legs from the 10.5cm le FH 18. Heavy and cumbersome but still very effective.

Note: Armor penetration figures are for standard armor-piercing, high-explosive shells (APHE), not tungsten core, discarding sabot ammunition.

GERMAN SELF-PROPELLED ARTILLERY

Type	Maximum Armor	Caliber	Weight of Shell	Rate of Fire	Maximum Range	Speed (km/h) and range	Comments
15cm sIG33(Sf) auf Pz.Kpfw. I Ausf B	13mm	15cm	38.0kg/83.8lb	2–3rpm	4,600m/5,030yd	40/140	Based on Panzer I chassis, 38 produced in 1940. Some still in service in 1943.
Leichte Feldhaubitze 18/2 auf Fahrgestell Pz.Kpfw II (Sf) "Wespe" Sd.Kfz. 124	30mm	10.5cm	14.81kg/32.66lb	4–6rpm	13,500m/14,764yd	40/220	Based on Panzer II chassis. Issued to the self-propelled artillery detachments of Panzer and Panzergrenadier divisions, entered service mid-1943.
15cm Schweres Infanteriegeschütz 33 (Sf) auf Pz.Kpfw. 38(t) Ausf H Sd.Kfz. 138/1 "Grille"	50mm	15cm	38.0kg/83.8lb	2–3rpm	4,600m/5,030yd	35/185	Based on the Panzer 38(t) chassis. Issued to the heavy infantry gun companies of Panzergrenadier regiments. A total of 90 produced.
15cm Schweres Infanteriegeschütz 33/1 (Sf) auf Selbstfahrlafette 38(t) Ausf K Sd.Kfz. 138/1 "Grille"	20mm	15cm	38.0kg/83.8lb	2–3rpm	4,600m/5,030yd	35/190	An improved variant with the howitzer mounted at the rear; 283 produced to September 1944.
Gepanzerter Selbstfahrlafette für Sturmgeschütz 7.5cm Kanone Ausf A-E Sd.Kfz. 142	50mm	7.5cm	6.0kg/13.23lb	6–8rpm	3,000m/3,281yd	40/160	Based on the Panzer III chassis. Intended as an infantry support vehicle with the low-velocity StuK 37 L/24 gun. A very successful vehicle used on all fronts from 1940. From the Ausf F version armed with a high-velocity StuK 40 L43/48 gun and used primarily as an antitank weapon.
10.5cm Sturmhaubitze 42 Sd.Kfz. 142/2	80mm	10.5cm	14.81kg/32.66lb	4–5rpm	7,800m/8,530yd	40/155	Direct fire support vehicle mounting the StuH42 L/24 gun.
Sturminfanteriegeschütz 33B	80mm	15cm	38.0kg/83.8lb	2–3rpm	4,600m/5,030yd	20/110	Based on Panzer III chassis with a fully-enclosed fighting compartment; 24 built.
15cm Schwere Panzerhaubitze auf Geschützwagen III/IV (Sf) "Hummel" Sd.Kfz. 165	30mm	15cm	43.5kg/95.92lb	4rpm	12,250m/13,397yd	42/215	Utilized a modified Panzer III/IV chassis. A very successful design in great demand. Issued to the heavy batteries of armored artillery detachments of Panzer divisions. A total of 724 were produced.
Sturmpanzer IV "Brummbär" Sd.Kfz. 166	100mm	15cm	38.0kg/83.8lb	2–3rpm	4,600m/5,030yd	40/210	A heavily armored assault tank based mainly on the Panzer IV Ausf G/J chassis. A total of 306 were produced/converted.

SOVIET SELF-PROPELLED ARTILLERY

Type	Maximum Armor	Caliber	Weight of Shell	Rate of Fire	Maximum Range	Speed (km/h) and range	Comments
KV-2	110mm	152mm	40kg/88.18lb	1–2rpm	10,000m/10,936yd	26/150	Variant of the KV-1 tank, heavily armored but too heavy and not very maneuverable.
SU-76M	35mm	76.2mm	6.23kg/13.73lb	10–12rpm	13,000m/14,217yd	45/190	In service in late 1943/44 based on the T-70 chassis. Not a success as an antitank weapon but a reliable fire support vehicle. Second to T-34 in numbers produced.
SU-122	45mm	122mm	22.6kg/49.82	2–3rpm	12,100m/13,233yd	45/190	A direct fire weapon based on the T-34 chassis. In service January 1944. Antitank performance was disappointing but the HE shell was devastating.
SU-152	60mm	152mm	40kg/88.18lb	1–2rpm	12,400m/13,561yd	45/190	In service 1943; developed as a tank destroyer but mainly used in the fire support role.

Note: This table lists the major German and Soviet fully-tracked self-propelled artillery weapons. Self-propelled antitank/dual-purpose weapons are not included.

SOVIET ARTILLERY

Type	Caliber	Weight of Shell	Rate of Fire	Armor Penetration 30 deg. from vertical	Maximum Range	Comments
Infantry Support Artillery						
76mm Polkavaya Pushka obr. 1927	76.2mm	6.4kg/14.1lb	14rpm	N/A	8,550m/9,350yd	A simple and robust weapon, large numbers produced. Extensive German use.
Mountain Arillery						
76.2mm Gornaya Pushka obr. 1909	76.2mm	6.23kg/13.73lb	10–12rpm	N/A	8,550m/9,350yd	Export version of the Schneider-Danglis 06/09, Tsarist weapons modernized in the 1930s.
76.2mm Gornaya Pushka obr. 1938	76.2mm	6.23kg/13.73lb	10rpm	N/A	10,100m/11,045yd	Czech 1936 design, license-built version in service with Soviet forces in 1938. Captured guns used by German mountain troops.
Field Artillery						
76mm Pushka obr. 1902/30 L/30	76.2mm	6.4kg/14.1lb	8rpm	N/A	12,400m/13,561yd	1930s modernization of old Tsarist guns. In large-scale service with Soviet Army in 1941. L/40 was a longer barreled modification. Both variants used by German artillery detachments.
76mm Pushka obr. 1902/30 L/40	76.2mm	6.4kg/14.1lb	8rpm	N/A	13,000m/14,217yd	
76mm Pushka obr. 1936 (F-22)	76.2mm	6.4kg/14.1lb	15rpm	500m–70mm	13,580m/14,851yd	Long barreled field gun with antitank capability. Large numbers captured by Germans, many converted to antitank guns 1942/43.
76mm Pushka obr. 1939 (USV)	76.2mm	6.4kg/14.1lb	15rpm	500m–70mm	13,290m/14,534yd	Dual-purpose field gun, lighter and more mobile than 76-36. Large numbers in German service with muzzle brake added.
76mm Pushka obr. 1942/ZIS-3 ('76-42)	76.2mm	6.21kg/13.69lb	15rpm	500m–80mm	13,000m/14,217yd	Excellent dual-purpose gun. 76-39 gun with a muzzle brake and a new split-trail carriage. Entered service 1942, large numbers produced.
107mm Pushka obr. 1910/30 107-10/30	107mm	17.18kg/37.87lb	5–6rpm	N/A	16,350m/17,880yd	Modernized Tsarist gun with longer barrel. Large numbers in service at Corps level. Captured examples used by regular German detachments.
Heavy Artillery						
122mm Gaubitsa obr. 1910/30 - 1909/37	121.92mm	21.76kg/47.97lb	6–7rpm	N/A	8,940m/9,777yd	French Schneider 10 S howitzer imported prior to WWI. Modernized in 1930s. Large numbers used by the Germans on the Eastern Front.
122mm Pushka obr. 1931 (122-31)	121.92mm	25kg/55.12lb	5–6rpm	N/A	20,870m/22,824yd	Soviet design of new barrel with carriage of 152mm gun-howitzer 1934 carriage. Rugged and very effective. Captured guns incorporated into German regular artillery detachments. 1931/37 model used carriage of 1937 152mm model gun-howitzer.
122mm Pushka obr. 1931/37 (A-19)	121.92mm	25kg/55.12lb	5–6rpm	N/A	20,400m/22,310yd	
122mm Gaubitsa obr. 1938 (M-30)	121.92mm	21.76kg/47.97lb	5–6rpm	500m–140mm	12,100m/13,233yd	One of the best artillery pieces of WWII. Entered service in 1938 and produced in large numbers. The numerous captured examples served with regular German artillery detachments and were also used as coastal artillery.
152mm Pushka obr. 1910/34	152.4mm	43.5kg/95.9lb	2–3rpm	N/A	17,600m/19,248yd	Interim design to produce a modern heavy gun. First used during Soviet-Finnish War, 1939–40. Large numbers captured by Germans 1941–42.
152mm Gaubitsa-Pushka obr. 1937 (ML-20)	152.4mm	43.5kg/95.9lb	2–3rpm	N/A	17,265m/18,881yd	Modern gun-howitzer designed primarily for counter-battery fire. 152mm 1910/34 barrel and 122mm 1931/37 carriage.
152mm Gaubitsa obr. 1938 (M-10)	152.4mm	51.1kg/112.66lb	2–4rpm	500m–200mm	12,400m/13,561yd	Reliable and efficient weapon with antitank capabilities. Entered service in 1938 and produced on a large scale. Captured guns used by German heavy artillery detachments. Improved version (D-1) introduced in 1943.
203mm Gaubitsa obr. 1931 (B-4)	203.2mm	100kg/220.46lb	1 round every 4 mins	N/A	18,025m/19,712yd	Introduced in service in 1932, an unusual but effective gun. Produced in 6 slightly different variants, including a fully tracked carriage.

SOVIET ARTILLERY *continued*

Type	Caliber	Weight of Shell	Rate of Fire	Armor Penetration 30 deg. from vertical	Maximum Range	Comments
Antiaircraft/Dual-Purpose Artillery						
37mm Zenitnaya Pushka obr. 1939	37mm	0.785kg/lb	80rpm practical	N/A	3,000m/3,281yd Maximum ceiling	Based off a 25mm Bofors design. Rugged and simple to operate. Captured guns fitted with German fire control equipment.
76.2mm Zenitnaya Pushka obr. 1931	76.2mm	6.61kg/14.57lb	15–20rpm	N/A	9,300m/10,171yd Maximum ceiling	Initial Soviet heavy AA gun. Large numbers in service in 1941 and many captured by Germans. Numerous guns rebored to 8.8cm caliber.
76.2mm Zenitnaya Pushka obr. 1938	76.2mm	6.61kg/14.57lb	15–20rpm	N/A	9,300m/10,171yd Maximum ceiling	Improved version of 1931 model gun. Large numbers in service in 1941 and many captured by Germans. Numerous guns rebored to 8.8cm caliber.
85mm Zenitnaya Pushka obr. 1939 (KS-12)	85mm	9.2kg/20.28lb	15–20rpm	1,000m–90mm	10,500m/11,483yd Maximum ceiling	Dual-purpose gun, very well designed. Equivalent to German *Flak 18/36*.
Antitank Artillery						
45mm Provitotankovaya Pushka obr. 1930/32	45mm	1.43kg/3.15lb	14rpm	500m–78mm 1,000m–37mm	4,670m/5,107yd (HE) 3,000m/3,281yd (AP)	A scaled-up version of the German *3.7cm PaK 35/36*. The 1937 model had a longer barrel and was used until 1945. Numerous guns in German service.
57mm Provitotankovaya Pushka obr. 1941 (ZiS-2)	57mm	4.2kg/9.26lb	14rpm	500m–140mm 1,000m–65mm	4,000m/4,374yd (AP) 5,200m/5,687yd (HE)	Very effective antitank/field gun introduced in mid-1941 and used throughout the war. Captured guns used by Germans until the end of the war.

Note: See also 76mm dual-purpose field guns

BIBLIOGRAPHY

Adamczyk, Werner. *Feuer! An Artilleryman's Life on the Eastern Front.* Wilmington, NC: Broadfoot, 1992.

Angolia, John R., and Adolf Schlicht. *Uniforms and Traditions of the German Army, 1933–1945.* Vol. 1–3. San Jose, CA: R. J. Bender, 1992.

Bernard, Georges, and Francois de Lannoy. *Les Divisions de L'Armee de Terre allemande Heer 1939–1945.* Bayeux, France: Editions Heimdal, 1997.

Bidermann, Gottlob Herbert. *In Deadly Combat: A German Soldier's Memoir of the Eastern Front.* Lawrence, KS: University Press of Kansas, 2000.

Buchner, Alex. *The German Infantry Handbook, 1939–1945.* Atglen, PA: Schiffer, 1991.

Carell, Paul. *Hitler's War on Russia: The Story of the German Defeat in the East.* London: Harrap, 1964.

Chamberlain, Peter, and Hilary Doyle. *Encyclopedia of German Tanks of World War.* Revised Edition. London: Arms and Armour Press, 1975.

DiNardo, R. L. *Mechanized Juggernaut or Military Anachronism?* Westport, CT: Greenwood Publishing, 1991.

Ellis, Chris, ed. *Directory of Wheeled Vehicles of the Wehrmacht.* London: Ducimus Books, 1974.

Ericson, John. *The Road to Stalingrad.* New York: Harper & Row, 1975.

Fritz, Stephen G. *Frontsoldaten.* Lexington, KY: University Press of Kentucky, 1995.

Gander, Terry, and Peter Chamberlain. *Small Arms, Artillery and Special Weapons of the Third Reich.* London: Macdonald and Jane's, 1978.

Guderian, Heinz. *Panzer Leader.* London: M. Joseph, 1970.

Hogg, Ian V. *German Artillery of World War Two.* London: Arms and Armour, 1977.

Kershaw, Robert J. *War without Garlands: Operation Barbarossa, 1941–1942.* Shepperton, England: Ian Allan, 2000.

Knappe, Siegfried, and Ted Brusaw. *Soldat: Reflections of a German Soldier, 1936–1949.* New York: Orion Books, 1992.

Le Tissier, Tony. *The Battle of Berlin 1945.* New York: St. Martins Press, 1988.

Lucas, James. *War on the Eastern Front, 1941–1945: The German Soldier in Russia.* London: Jane's, 1979.

Luck, Hans von. *Panzer Commander.* New York: Praeger, 1989.

Metelmann, Henry. *Through Hell for Hitler.* Havertown, PA: Casemate, 2001.

Porter, David. *Order of Battle: The Red Army in WWII.* London: Amber Books, 2009.

The Research Institute for Military History. *Germany and the Second World War.* Vol. IV: *The Attack on the Soviet Union.* Oxford, England: Clarendon Press, 1998.

Seaton, Albert. *The Russo-German War: 1941–45.* Novato, CA: Presidio Press, 1990.

Smith J. R., and Anthony Kay. *German Aircraft of the Second World War.* London: Putnam, 1972.

Stahlberg, Alexander. *Bounden Duty: The Memoirs of a German Officer: 1932–45.* London: Brassey's, 1990.

Tsouras, Peter G., ed. *Fighting in Hell: The German Ordeal on the Eastern Front.* London: Greenhill, 1995.

———. *Panzers on the Eastern Front: General Erhard Raus and His Panzer Divisions in Russia, 1941–1945.* London: Greenhill, 2002.

U.S. War Department. *Handbook on German Military Forces.* Baton Rouge, LA: Louisiana State University Press, 1990.

Wray, Maj. Timothy A. *Standing Fast: German Defensive Doctrine on the Russian Front During World War II Prewar to March 1943.* Kansas: Combat Studies Institute, 1986.

Zaloga, Steven J., and James Grandsen. *Soviet Tanks and Combat Vehicles of World War Two.* London: Arms and Armour Press, 1984.

———. *The Eastern Front Armor Camouflage and Markings, 1941 to 1945.* London: Arms and Armour Press, 1989.

Ziemke, Earl F., and Magna E. Bauer. *Moscow to Stalingrad.* New York: Military Heritage Press, 1988.

ACKNOWLEDGMENTS

The following people deserve credit for their generous assistance in supplying period photographs taken by the combatants themselves, along with modern color images of uniforms, equipment, and weapons. In each and every case, they went above and beyond to help bring this book to life by offering their expertise and time: Pat Cassidy, Steve Cassidy, P. Whammond and Carey of Collector's Guild (www.germanmilitaria.com), Wilson History and Research Center (www.militaryheadgear.com), Jim Haley, David A. Jones, Jim Pool, Scott Pritchett, Phil Francis, Paul Wills, and Aleks and Dmitri of Espenlaub Militaria (www. aboutww2militaria.com and www.warrelics.eu/forum), as well as the National Archives, the Swedish Army Museum, and a few individuals who wish to remain anonymous.